Black Cowboys

Ryan P. Randolph

The Rosen Publishing Group's
PowerKids Press™
New York

To my wife, Joanne, thank you for everything

Published in 2003 by The Rosen Publishing Group, Inc.
29 East 21st Street, New York, NY 10010

First Edition

Managing Editor: Kathy Kuhtz Campbell
Book Designer: Emily Muschinske

Photo Credits: Cover and title page, p. 21 (left) © Denver Public Library, Colorado Historical Society and Denver Art Museum; back cover, pp. 9 (left), 13 (bottom), 21 (right) © Western History Collections, University of Oklahoma Libraries; p. 5 © The Erwin E. Smith Collection of the Library of Congress on deposit at the Amon Carter Museum, Ft. Worth, TX; p. 5 (inset) © Hulton/Archive/Getty Images; pp. 6, 13 (top), 17 (right), 18 (right), 21 (inset) © William Loren Katz Collection; p. 6 (inset) © Christie's Images/CORBIS; pp. 9 (right), 10, 14 © North Wind Picture Archives; pp. 17 (left) © Bettmann/CORBIS; p. 18 (left) © Jonathan Blair/CORBIS.

Manufactured in the United States of America

Contents

Black Explorers in the West

Cowboys played an important role in the history of America's West from the 1860s to the 1890s. They worked on the cattle trails in today's states of Texas, New Mexico, Kansas, Montana, and Wyoming, among others. Many of these cowboys were Mexican, and many were African American, or black.

Blacks were involved in other areas of **exploration** in the American West. In 1803, a slave named York played an important part in Meriwether Lewis and William Clark's **expedition** to the Pacific Ocean. York hunted for food and spoke several languages, including French, to help the explorers on their long journey. The famous **mountain man** James Beckwourth was also an early black explorer of America's West. A hunter, a fur trapper, and an adventurer, Beckwourth served for many years as a scout for the U.S. Army before his death in 1866.

These black cowboys are wearing chaps, handkerchiefs called bandannas, and wide-brimmed hats. Inset: *James Beckwourth, seen here in a photo from the 1840s, found a way through the Sierra Nevadas. Today this route near Reno, Nevada, is called Beckwourth Pass.*

Black Cowboy Beginnings

In the southern United States before the **Civil War** began in 1861, one of the many tasks slaves had to do was to take care of cattle and horses on large estates, called plantations, and farms. In the 1830s and 1840s, slave owners brought slaves to the rich lands of southern Texas. Besides being ideal for growing cotton and corn, the wide-open range provided space for cattle to feed. At the time, ranchers raised cattle mostly for their hides, for making leather, and for tallow, or fat, for making soap and candles. The first black cowboys probably learned the arts of herding, **branding**, **breeding**, and roping cattle and taming horses from Mexican cowboys.

Ranchers needed skilled cowboys, such as Jessie Stahl, shown here, to tame horses. Inset: Mexican cowboys, called vaqueros *(from* vaca, *the Spanish word for cow), worked in Texas and New Mexico.*

DID YOU KNOW?

Before 1861, some skilled slaves trained racehorses. They also worked as jockeys. After the end of slavery, former slaves continued to be trainers and jockeys. A black rider won the first Kentucky Derby in 1875.

Cattle Becomes King

After the Civil War ended in 1865, the cattle industry grew. The demand for beef in the large cities in the East and the North increased with the population. People found new ways to package and refrigerate beef in these large cities.

Texas was not connected yet by railroad to places in the North. To reach these new markets in the North, ranchers needed to drive, or walk, the cattle to **stockyards** near railroad routes. In 1867, cattle rancher Joseph McCoy helped to establish the Chisholm Trail, which started near San Antonio, Texas, and ran to Abilene, Kansas. McCoy worked with the Kansas Pacific Railroad to have the railroad connect at Abilene. It took about eight cowboys to drive a herd of 2,500 cattle. A cattle drive from southern Texas to Kansas could take about three months. Many blacks in Texas with skills in riding horses and working with animals fit the ranchers' demands for more cowboys to work on the cattle drives.

Above: The cowboys drove the cattle herds to towns called railheads, such as Abilene or Wichita, Kansas. In these towns, the cowboys herded the cattle into stockyards, such as this one in Kansas City, Missouri, and then loaded them into railroad cars that would take them to Chicago or other northern cities.

Left: In the early 1900s, cowboy Bill Pickett and his horse, Spradley, became experts at wrestling steers. A cowboy's horse was his most important tool. His rope was his next most important tool.

A Tough Job

Cowboy life was lonely and hard because of the many long months cowboys spent on the trail. As did blacks in other parts of the United States, black cowboys in the West faced **racism** and **discrimination**. However, because of the high demand for all cowboys, blacks and whites often got equal pay. No matter what their race or background, cowboys trusted one another with their lives, because life on the trail was dangerous. Equal pay and equal work meant that black and Mexican cowboys were treated more fairly than blacks and Mexicans were treated elsewhere in the nation.

A cowboy might spend 18 hours each day riding in the saddle. He rounded up cattle and branded them before starting the cattle drive.

DID YOU KNOW?

Although figures are not exact, there were from 5,000 to 9,500 black cowboys working in the West between 1870 and 1885. This means that during that period 25 percent of all cowboys might have been black.

Life on the Range

On the cattle drives to **cow towns**, such as the Kansas towns of Dodge City and Abilene, there was a trail boss, a cook, a team of cowboys to drive the cattle herds, and a **wrangler** who was in charge of the horses. The trail boss was in charge of the cattle from the time they left the ranch until they were sold. Black cowboys, no matter how talented, usually were not permitted to become trail bosses or owners of large ranches because of racism.

The wrangler was the lowest position on the trail, but he was in charge of about 50 horses, which the cowboys needed to drive the many cattle to the North. The cook drove the **chuck wagon**, which carried all the food on the trail. The wrangler and the cook usually traveled ahead of the herds and set up camp. Cowboys treated the cook with respect, because they did not want the cook to give them cold or bad food.

Judge Roy Bean, the "Law West of the Pecos," holding court at the old town of Langtry, Texas, in 1900, trying a horse thief. This building was courthouse and saloon. No other peace officers in the locality at that time.

Left: *Black cowboys got the same stern treatment from Judge Roy Bean, known as the Law West of the Pecos, as white cowboys.*

Bottom: *Cowboys ate meals at the chuck wagon. A chuck wagon held a water barrel, food, cooking tools, ropes, bedrolls, and a first-aid kit.*

Famous Cowboys: Bose Ikard

A few black cowboys, such as Bose Ikard, became famous. Ikard worked for Oliver Loving in 1866, and later worked for Charles Goodnight. Cattle ranchers Loving and Goodnight founded the Goodnight-Loving Trail. This trail ran from Texas through New Mexico to Colorado and Wyoming. In Texas, Ikard learned how to ride horses and drive cattle herds. He later became the most trusted of Goodnight's cowboys. Goodnight recalled, "There was a dignity, a cleanliness, and a reliability about him. His behavior was very good in a fight, and [he] was probably the most devoted man to me that I ever knew."

During a cattle drive, cowboys could work about 2,500 cattle into a column of four or five side by side that might stretch for 2 miles (3 km). Cowboys rode in the positions of point (head), flank (side), and drag (end).

DID YOU KNOW?

In 1809, in Folsom, New Mexico, cowboy George McJunkin found animal bones and handmade objects that proved Native Americans had been on the continent for about 10,000 years instead of the 3,000 years that scientists first believed.

Larger-than-Life Characters: Nat Love

Some black cowboys have a legendary, or larger-than-life, **legacy**. The life of Nat Love, also known as Deadwood Dick, is one example. Love said he received the **nickname** Deadwood Dick after winning several roping and shooting contests at a rodeo in Deadwood City, Dakota Territory.

His **autobiography**, *The Life and Adventures of Nat Love*, was published in 1907, and contained stories of his adventures. He was born a slave in Tennessee in 1854, and "struck out for Kansas" in 1869. For many years, he worked as a cowboy in the cattle drives between Texas and Kansas. Love wrote that black cowboys were welcome in saloons, theaters, and hotels of cow towns such as Dodge City as long as they had money. He recalled that once he rode a horse without a saddle for 100 miles (161 km). He also told about being shot 14 times during his life.

Right: *Nat Love, also known as Deadwood Dick, had many adventures as a cowboy. In his book, he wrote about riding in dangerous storms and fighting off raids by Native Americans.*
Far Right: *Legendary cowboy Bill Pickett became the first black cowboy movie star.*

Below: *The adventures of cattle rustlers, such as Isom Dart, and the cowboys and lawmen who chased them inspired writers of dime novels. This book about Arizona Joe, an adventurous cowboy, was popular in 1887.*

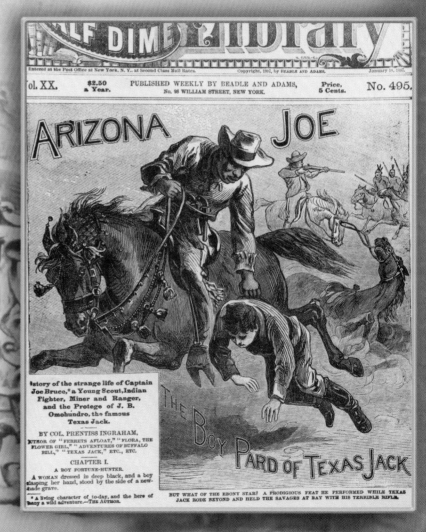

HALF DIME LIBRARY

Entered at the Post Office at New York, N. Y., at Second Class Mail Rates.   Copyright, 1887, by BEADLE AND ADAMS.   January 18, 1887.

Vol. XX. $2.50 a Year.   PUBLISHED WEEKLY BY BEADLE AND ADAMS, No. 98 WILLIAM STREET, NEW YORK.   Price, 5 Cents.   No. 495.

ARIZONA JOE

Story of the strange life of Captain Joe Bruce,* a Young Scout, Indian Fighter, Miner and Ranger, and the Protege of J. B. Omohundro, the famous Texas Jack.

BY COL. PRENTISS INGRAHAM,
AUTHOR OF "FERRETS AFLOAT," "FLORA, THE FLOWER GIRL," "ADVENTURES OF BUFFALO BILL," "TEXAS JACK," ETC., ETC.

CHAPTER I.
A BOY FORTUNE-HUNTER.

A WOMAN dressed in deep black, and a boy clasping her hand, stood by the side of a new-made grave.

* A living character of to-day, and the hero of many a wild adventure.—THE AUTHOR.

THE BOY PARD OF TEXAS JACK

BUT WHAT OF THE EBONY STAR? A PRODIGIOUS FEAT HE PERFORMED WHILE TEXAS JACK RODE BEYOND AND HELD THE SAVAGES AT BAY WITH HIS TERRIBLE RIFLE.

Cattle Rustlers and Horse Thieves: Isom Dart

Not all cowboys stayed honest all the time. One such cowboy was Ned Huddleston, better known as Isom Dart. Born a slave in Arkansas, Ned moved to Texas after 1865. Next he went to Mexico, where he stole horses with a partner. Then he came back to the United States. He tried life as a miner and a cook, but ended up stealing horses and cattle in Colorado. Lawmen tracked down Ned's partners while he was away and killed them. Ned changed his name to Isom Dart and fled to Oklahoma. Later, in Wyoming, he was arrested for stealing cattle.

Left: A photographer took this picture of Isom Dart in Brown's Park, Utah, which is located on the Outlaw Trail. The Outlaw Trail was a route that led from Mexico to Canada.

DID YOU KNOW?

It was unusual for cowboys to be found guilty of cattle rustling. Isom Dart tamed wild horses for ranchers and built up his own ranch. On October 3, 1900, Tom Horn, a hired killer, was said to have slain Dart after other ranchers had accused Dart of stealing their cattle.

Wild West Shows and Rodeos

By the 1890s, the building of railroads throughout the West lessened the demand for cowboys and cattle drives to cow towns in the North. Cattle ranchers could ship their cattle to stockyards by train. These ranchers no longer needed as many cowboys to work on their ranches. Black cowboys, such as Jesse Stahl and Bill Pickett, found new work riding horses, roping cattle, and shooting guns in rodeos and Wild West shows. Stahl gained fame as a **broncobuster**. Pickett had worked as a cowboy for many years. Around 1900, Pickett invented steer wrestling, also called **bulldogging**. In the 1880s, William "Buffalo Bill" Cody's Wild West show traveled throughout the United States and in Europe with **sharpshooting** acts and special roping events. Traveling shows such as William Cody's gave people an idea of what life was like in America's Wild West.

Bill Pickett was often billed as the Dusky Demon at rodeos. He died on April 2, 1932, after being kicked in the head by a horse on the 101 Ranch in Oklahoma. Inset: A poster from around 1915 tells about the silent movie in which Pickett performed his bulldogging feats.

BILL PICKETT, FAMOUS NEGRO COWBOY

FIRST MAN BULLDOGGER

ALSO USED HIS TEETH BULL DOGGING INSTEAD OF HANDS ON HORNS METHOD USED BY COWBOYS TODAY

Pickett's trick of biting into a steer's nose or lip to wrestle it, the way a dog might, made him the first bulldogger.

THE NORMAN FILM MFG. CO.
PRESENTS

BILL PICKETT
WORLD'S COLORED CHAMPION...
'THE BULL-DOGGER'
Featuring The Colored Hero of the Mexican Bull Ring
in Death Defying Feats of Courage and Skill.
THRILLS! LAUGHS TOO!
Produced by NORMAN FILM MFG. CO.
JACKSONVILLE, FLA.

The Legacy of Black Cowboys

Texas-born Bill Pickett worked with the Miller brothers from 1905 to 1931. The Millers took the cowboys who worked on their 101 Ranch in Ponca City, Oklahoma, and had them perform in a Wild West show in New York City, Mexico City, and London. Pickett died in 1932. In 1971, he was the first black to be admitted to the National Cowboy and Western Heritage Museum's Rodeo Hall of Fame in Oklahoma City, Oklahoma.

As the need for cattle drives and cowboys along the cattle trails of the West died out, most novels, movies, and historians described all cowboys and settlers in the West as being white. In fact black cowboys were a large part of the population of cowboys. The Black American West Museum and Heritage Center in Denver, Colorado, continues to offer a view of the history, culture, and legacy of blacks in the West.

Glossary

autobiography (ah-toh-by-AH-gruh-fee) The story of a person's life, written by that person.

branding (BRAND-ing) Burning with a hot iron to mark something to show ownership.

breeding (BREED-ing) Bringing a male animal and a female animal together to have babies.

broncobuster (BRAHN-koh-bus-ter) A person who breaks in wild horses to the saddle.

bulldogging (BUL-dog-ing) Grabbing a bull by the horns and turning its head sideways so that the bull stops and lowers its head to the ground.

chuck wagon (CHUK WA-gen) A wagon that carries food and supplies.

Civil War (SIH-vul WOR) The war fought between the Northern and Southern states of America from 1861 to 1865.

cow towns (KOW TOWNZ) Towns that serve as a market center or shipping point for cattle.

discrimination (dis-krih-muh-NAY-shun) Treating a person badly or unfairly just because that person is different.

expedition (ek-spuh-DIH-shun) A group of people on a trip for a special purpose.

exploration (ek-spluh-RAY-shun) Traveling over little-known land.

legacy (LEH-guh-see) Something left behind by a person's actions.

mountain man (MOWN-tun MAN) A man who hunted beavers in the Rocky Mountains during the early 1800s.

nickname (NIK-naym) A funny or interesting name that is used instead of a person's real name.

racism (RAY-sih-zum) The belief that one group or race or group of people, such as whites, is better than another group, such as blacks.

sharpshooting (SHARP-shoot-ing) Shooting with great accuracy, or skill.

stockyards (STAHK-yardz) Fenced-in areas near trains or other transportation where animals wait before being shipped to another place.

wrangler (RAYN-geh-ler) A ranch hand who takes care of the saddle horses.

Index

B
Beckwourth, James, 4
branding, 7
breeding, 7

C
Chisholm Trail, 8
Civil War, 7, 8
Cody, William "Buffalo Bill," 20
cook, 12, 19

G
Goodnight, Charles, 15

H
Huddleston, Ned (Isom Dart), 19

I
Ikard, Bose, 15

L
Love, Nat (Deadwood Dick), 16
Loving, Oliver, 15

M
Mexican (cowboys), 4, 7, 11

P
Pickett, Bill, 20, 22

R
ranch(es), 12, 20, 22
rancher(s), 7, 8, 12, 15, 20
rodeo(s), 16, 22

T
Texas, 4, 7, 8, 15, 16, 19
trail boss, 12

W
Wild West show(s), 20, 22
wrangler, 12

Y
York, 4

Primary Sources

Page 5 (inset). *James Pierson Beckwourth.* This photograph of the well-known mountain man was taken around 1840, before Beckwourth established a trading post in 1842 that later became the city of Pueblo, Colorado. **Page 5.** *Black Cowpunchers.* Cowboys were also called cowpunchers. This undated photograph shows a group of cowboys attending a fair in Bonham, Texas. **Page 6.** *Jessie Stahl.* An undated photo shows cowboy Jessie Stahl riding his horse, Glass Eye, in a rodeo in Salinas, California. Stahl invented hoolihanding, or ramming a steer's horns into the ground during rodeo competitions. Today this method is no longer allowed at rodeos. **Page 6 (inset).** *A Vaquero.* Artist Frederic Remington, who worked as a cowboy in the West, painted this picture of a Mexican cowboy sometime between 1881 and 1909. **Page 9 (left).** *Bill Pickett at a Rodeo Performance.* An undated photograph captures bulldogger Bill Pickett riding his horse, Spradley, before a rodeo performance. The image is in the collection of William Loren Katz, who wrote a history book, *The Black West*, to document the African American role in the westward expansion of the United States. **Page 9 (above).** *A Stockyard in Kansas City, Missouri.* This 1890s photo shows a drover with a herd of cattle. **Page 10.** *The Herd at Night.* This picture is a hand-colored woodcut by Frederic Remington. **Page 13 (left).** *The Jersey Lilly.* This photo shows the saloon where Judge Roy Bean held court. He helped found the town of Langtry, Texas, where the saloon is located, and named both the town and the saloon after the English actress Lillie Langtry. A colorful figure, Bean was not trained as a judge, but became the justice of the peace of the region, the "Law West of the Pecos." **Page 13 (bottom).** *Cowboys Eat Around a Chuck Wagon.* This photo of cowboys on a Texas trail was taken around 1885. Black cowboys were usually a part of every Texas cattle drive. **Page 17 (left).** *Nat Love, Deadwood Dick.* This studio photograph of the popular black cowboy Nat Love was taken sometime between 1876 and 1890. **Page 18 (left).** *Ned Huddleston, Isom Dart.* Jonathan Blair took this photo of Dart when Dart had stopped at Brown's Park, Utah, on the Outlaw Trail. The Outlaw Trail ran from Mexico to Canada. **Page 18 (right).** *Arizona Joe, the Boy Pard of Texas Jack.* A five-cent Western novel from 1887 shows that a black cowboy was a popular subject for readers. **Page 21 (left).** *Bill Pickett.* This photo shows Pickett with a lariat, or rope, which he excelled in using during his cowhand days at the 101 Ranch in Oklahoma. **Page 21 (inset).** *Poster of Bill Pickett.* This poster advertises the silent picture Pickett, the first bulldogger, starred in around the time of World War I.

Web Sites

Due to the changing nature of Internet links, PowerKids Press has developed an online list of Web sites related to the subject of this book. This site is updated regularly. Please use this link to access the list: www.powerkidslinks.com/lwe/blcow/